Also by JD Viharini

*Enjoying India: The Essential Handbook*

# Travel Fearlessly in India

*What Every Woman Should Know About Personal Safety*

*JD Viharini*

Enjoying India Guides

Seattle 2016

www.tarasatarapress.com
ISBN: 978-0-9819503-5-8



*Although the author and publisher have made every effort to present accurate and up-to-date information in this book with utmost care and diligence, and have made every effort to ensure the accuracy and completeness of the information contained within, we assume no responsibility for errors, inaccuracies, omissions or inconsistencies. This book includes information that has been gathered from personal experience as well as many other sources. It is published for general reference and is not intended to be a substitute for independent verification by readers when necessary and appropriate. This book is sold with the understanding that the publisher and the author are not engaged in rendering legal, medical or other professional advice. The publisher and author disclaim any personal liability, either directly or indirectly, for advice presented within.*

# Table of Contents

# PREFACE

When I first came to India as a tourist in 2000, I was more concerned about getting sick or being scammed than rape or sexual harassment. I researched Indian culture thoroughly before my trip, took precautions, and made sure I dressed in a conservative and smart manner. I was generally treated respectfully and, much to my surprise, even complimented on my attire. However, these days, a growing number of negative media reports about incidents of sexual violence and misconduct in India have created overwhelming safety fears in women's minds.

Personally, I don't feel that India is unsafe for foreign women. It's uncomfortable at times, yes, but not particularly unsafe. Yet, lack of awareness and understanding of Indian culture often unwittingly make foreign women a target of it.

I've lived in India since 2005 and have explored much of the country during the course of my work, writing and managing the content for About.com's India travel website. I'm also married to an Indian man. This has given me some excellent insights into Indian culture. Nevertheless, it's taken me years to unravel it — and I'm still learning! There are major differences in the way men and women interact in India compared to the west, and the ways I've had to adapt my dress and behavior don't come naturally but are necessary.

Rather than minimizing India's issues and focusing only on the positives, as some writers tend to do, I believe the key is to have realistic expectations and unbiased information. Know what you're likely to encounter and how to deal with it! This will remove fear and give you confidence.

Hence, a practical book about Indian culture is an invaluable resource for foreign women when visiting India. And, I can't think of a better person to write such a book than J D Viharini, a single American woman who's been living in India for more than a decade. She visited India for the first time in 1980 and since then has traveled extensively throughout most of the country by herself, using all modes and classes of transportation, and staying in all types of accommodations (from "Ritz to the pits", as she says). Not only does she know what it's like to travel solo as a foreign woman, she's developed great insight into Indian culture and how the country functions at all levels.

I greatly admire how J D Viharini has integrated herself into Indian society, and the way she shares the vastness and diversity of her experiences. Her life in India has not been insular. She's spent time staying with traditional Indian families and in poor villages. As a result, she's developed a profound and deep understanding of India and Indian culture, which is reflected in her book.

Women's safety is a sensitive topic, and as J D Viharini pertinently points out, "unfortunately quite a few people have the idea that cultural requirements of modesty are a justification for victim-blaming." It's easy to underestimate the importance of dress and respect in Indian culture, especially when Indian women can frequently be seen wearing shorts, skirts, and sleeveless tops in major Indian cities. However, as the book explains in detail, this does not reflect the values of the conservative majority.

*Travel Fearlessly in India, What Every Woman Should Know About Personal Safety* is a remarkably comprehensive, sensible, and astute book that's packed full of perceptive information, tips and strategies. It covers everything from the mindsets of Indian men and how they conduct themselves to what you need to do if you have to go to the police. It's a book every female should read, and reread, before traveling to India.

— Sharell Cook
India Travel Specialist for About.com and
author of *Henna for the Broken Hearted*

# INTRODUCTION

You *can* travel safely in India with confidence, even if you are going solo. However, India's many cultures—and there are a huge number of diverse cultures within this amazing land—are entirely different than anything most visitors have experienced elsewhere, so you do need a good understanding of what's what to be able to function well and feel safe here.

This book is primarily for women and girls traveling to India, as well as those who have decided to stay for a while, whether solo or not. Though the practical recommendations in this book are no less helpful for Indian girls, many of the explanations are specifically for non-Indians. Also, there are a number of issues Indian girls may have to face—especially concerning relatives and neighbors—that are not applicable to visitors and which are outside the scope of this book.

My aim is to inspire you and give you the knowledge you need to travel in India with confidence. By knowing what to expect and how to prevent problems, you can remove constant anxieties and fears about sexual harassment and rape from the equation.[1] That's no guarantee that you'll never be afraid. There could be times when it may be appropriate and even necessary to feel afraid. But never let your fears control you.

The focus of this book is on preventing problems, which is by far the most important aspect of self-defense. Most of us are not martial arts experts who know how to effectively defend ourselves in a physical conflict. Real self-defense is not about defending yourself physically—it's about knowing how to avoid getting into in a physical conflict in the first place. While much of the advice in this book would apply anywhere, there are many points that are specific to India.

Naturally, many of the tips in this book may be considered common sense—but the 'common' part is abit questionable—there are a lot of things that people may fail to consider until something actually happens. You might say, "Well, that seems obvious"—but have you really thought about it before, and have you ever actually done it? If not, then maybe it isn't quite so obvious after all.

You are unlikely to need all the tips and strategies in this book. Getting obsessed with trying to do everything right all the time would ruin your trip. Figure

[1] To learn more about what to expect in India with respect to other considerations such as health and social interactions, see *Enjoying India: The Essential Handbook.*

out what is essential to make you feel comfortable and safe wherever you happen to be at any given time. There may be times and places where you need to do more, so it's good to know how to take maximum precautions even if you may never need them.

If you ask an Indian about the situation in the area where they live, among people from similar social and economic backgrounds as their own, you usually get reliable information. Beyond that sphere, however, their answers to your questions are likely to be unreliable.

Do ask your Indian friends about safety, but consider their answers in the appropriate context. For instance, if you ask someone from Bangalore about a village in Madhya Pradesh, you are unlikely to get a useful answer because they are extremely different places. Even in the same city, there are major differences. Asking someone who lives in one of the wealthy enclaves about an area that caters to budget travelers—or vice versa—is not likely to give you an accurate feel for the situation. They are completely different worlds.

India will challenge every mental and emotional boundary you have. There's no doubt about that. Many boundaries will be stretched; some might get shattered to pieces. But it's a good thing because that's what growth is all about. Go ahead and let your boundaries be annihilated. The greatest rewards in life are on the other side of fear.

Don't waste your energy worrying. Don't be ruled by fear. You don't have to be scared of traveling in India. Instead, learn what you need to know; cultivate the right demeanor and attitude; develop good habits; and then get on with enjoying your time in India!

## TRAVELING FEARLESSLY

There are basically two different kinds of fear. One kind of fear is that instinctive fear which arises in response to present or immanent danger, such as anyone would experience when coming face to face with an angry grizzly bear. Fear brings on the fight or flight response that is appropriate when we are faced with a serious immediate threat to our life and wellbeing. This kind of natural fear is necessary to our survival.

The kind of fear that doesn't serve any useful purpose in our lives is the fear of something that isn't present, of something that hasn't happened, of something that isn't even likely to happen, of something that might not even exist except in our own mind. That's the kind of fear that keeps us from traveling, from doing things we'd like to do, from expanding our boundaries, from going against expectations imposed by others. That kind of fear we don't need in our lives.

Knowledge is a great weapon against this kind of psychological fear—and this is the kind of fearlessness we need to cultivate when we travel. In this book, you will learn how to avoid becoming a victim of violence. You will also learn how to prevent or minimize non-threatening harassment and how to deal with it. When you feel secure, you don't worry. Whenever you feel you have taken sufficient measures to prevent something bad from happening, you stop worrying about it, don't you?

Even if you find you can't completely stop worrying about something that hasn't happened, try to conquer your fear and go ahead anyway. Don't let it control you. You don't ever want to be paralyzed by fear. So fearlessness doesn't necessarily mean you never feel fear. It's the ability to go ahead in spite of it.

Traveling fearlessly in India with respect to personal safety is mainly a matter of knowledge and preparation. It's all about confidence that's grounded in knowledge and in reality, not wishful thinking.

Now, a slight digression, as I can't resist taking the subject of fearlessness to its ultimate end. The Upanishads state that "fear arises from duality", and that "Self-realization alone makes one fearless."[2]

---

[2] Brihadaranyaka Upanishad 1.4.2-3.

Supreme enlightenment, *brahmicetana,* Brahman Consciousness, is a state where everything is experienced in terms of one's own unbounded Self. Indeed, everything is one's Self. That is the only true, unrestricted fearlessness. All other states of fearlessness can only be partial. Every unenlightened being experiences fear of one sort or another. OK, enough of that.

Fearless is not the same as complacent. It doesn't mean clinging blindly to a "nothing will happen" attitude. Nor does it mean throwing caution to the wind and taking risks. What it does mean is freedom from unnecessary worry because you've prepared yourself in advance.

## HOW SAFE IS INDIA?

Given the recent news from India, you might have the impression that India is an incredibly dangerous place for women to travel. That's just not true. Although, as anywhere else, women have to exercise a certain amount of care and vigilance, violent crime against non-Indians is rare. If you come to India knowing the essentials of staying safe—and if you are sensible, alert, and respectful of the culture—there is little risk of being the victim of sexual violence.

Fear of rape is simply not a reason to avoid India. Looking at the facts, you can see that you are probably safer from violent crime here than in your own country.[3]

Every attack on a non-Indian woman makes the headlines in a big way, but don't be put off by the bad press. The number of reported rapes of non-Indians in India is actually fewer than 1 in 100,000. Compare that with the US, for instance, where more than 24 rapes per 100,000 are reported. While we all know that many rapes are unreported in either country, this still gives a reasonable comparison.

Because the media likes to portray India as a particularly dangerous place for women to visit, it's necessary to put the risk factor in perspective. This is not to deny that there is a problem (though it's a global one, not just an Indian problem) or to trivialize it in any way. The sole upside of so much negative press is that the outrage of Indians is starting to bring about much-needed changes of attitudes, in addition to positive action on the part of the government.

---

3 "India's 'Rape Epidemic': An Ugly Colonial Myth Reborn", Sadhvi Sharma,
http://www.spiked-online.com/newsite/article/indias-rape-epidemic-an-ugly-colonial-myth-reborn/16781

Men should behave decently; but since some don't, we have to protect ourselves. While violent assault is pretty rare, other forms of sexual harassment are not so uncommon. In any case, if you are careful and sensible and project a confident, fearless attitude, you are not likely to run into serious problems. Most violent crimes against non-Indian women in India are preventable and much harassment can be avoided.

What level of precautions you need to take depends on who you are with or if you are alone; where you are going; when you will be there; and any special events that may be going on at the time.

Personal safety is always a bigger issue for women than men, although it's possible for even single women to travel around India alone without being constantly harassed. However, India is as diverse in attitudes towards women as in everything else, a fact you have to be aware of. Some places are really safe, while others may require you to use maximum precautions to feel safe. Find out about places before you go there, and when you arrive, talk to the locals to get a feel for the situation.

The first time I came to India alone, I was nervous. Even though I already knew quite a lot about the culture and what I needed to do to stay safe, as I had been here several times before, I was worried because people kept telling me it wasn't safe to travel alone in India; I should only be with a group, etc. To my surprise, I quickly found that I felt much safer in India than in the US. Since that time, I have been living and traveling in India by myself for around thirteen years, but have never experienced more than occasional mild harassment, none of which was ever an actual threat.

## ABOUT INDIAN MEN...

Even though sexual harassment is not uncommon, especially in tourist areas, it's actually only a small percentage of men who go around harassing women. Most Indian men will help you and treat you with respect, especially if you present yourself as someone deserving it. But, unfortunately, you can't just forget about the others.

Since in India there are relatively few opportunities for sex outside of marriage, many men feel extreme sexual pressure and frustration, so it's foolish to unnecessarily inflame those feelings. Because the society is so conservative, Indian men can get aroused by modes of dress and behaviors that wouldn't get men excited in most other countries. The trouble is that if a man gets aroused by the way you dress or act, it's not just *his* problem. It becomes *your* problem if he treats you like a prostitute because he thinks you're inviting sex when you aren't.

It is quite common for Indian men to work far from their homes, in which case they may only see their wives once a month or even once a year, which adds significantly to their frustration. This is not only the case for unskilled and domestic workers, but for many who travel for business or who work in the tourism sector as well.

Instead of taking responsibility for their own behavior, men who are lacking in self-control often put forth the specious, self-serving excuse that women are weak because they can't resist trying to seduce men! An absurd argument, indeed, yet it is accepted by much of Indian society. But however unfair it is that men blame women for their own weaknesses, we can't ignore the fact that men can get easily aroused, and they don't always control their urges.

In addition to the men you are interacting with socially, there are many men present in the background that one tends not to even notice—servants, drivers, etc.—and they often come from traditional backgrounds, even if you encounter them in the most rarefied environments. This cultural context makes a huge difference and you can't ignore it, even if your cosmopolitan friends and associates like to believe that they themselves are completely disassociated from traditional Indian life. Moreover, many Indians simply do not consider those from the lower classes (i.e. the vast majority) in their thinking. They go about their lives without really seeing them.

The cultural norm in most of India is for women to keep a safe distance from men, especially strangers. Most Indian men wouldn't approach Indian girls as casually as they might approach non-Indians, because doing so would be seen as an insult. They may think it doesn't matter because we are unaware of the insult.

Most Indian men are brought up not to touch women accidentally. A hand brushing your breast or hip is usually deliberate.

Unfortunately, it's always necessary to be on your guard with men you don't know or are just getting to know, no matter how nice they seem. Sometimes the most charming ones are the worst con artists. You are more likely to meet up with men of this sort in the major tourist areas. There are always some who are out to get whatever they can. Indian men of this sort may view foreign women as a source of "safe" sex (safe in the sense that they can easily be kept away from family and friends who disapprove of sex outside marriage), or "sex education" (getting a bit of practice in before marriage), prestige, money or a ticket to another country.

Don't tell men you don't know well exactly where you are staying unless you want them knocking on your door—or maybe even climbing in the window.

Avoid interacting with groups of men, even to ask directions. Men who hang out in packs are often insecure and they may feel they have to prove something to their buddies.

But don't worry. This is not to say that you should never talk to Indian men. Not at all. Just be a bit cautious and use good sense. And don't ignore any feeling you might have that something is off.

## ...AND FELLOW TRAVELERS, TOO

Indian men are not the only ones you have to be concerned about. Be cautious with new friends you make in your travels, whether or not they are Indian. Most of us tend to gravitate towards others from our own or similar cultures as a refuge in an unfamiliar world, but that's not a reason to automatically trust them. Be friendly, but don't reveal too many details about yourself and your travel plans to people you don't know well—even other women.

The reality is that the majority of rapes in India, as in the West, are not committed by strangers. The culprits are more likely to be known to the victims.

Letting your guard down with any guy you don't know well, whether he's Indian or from your own country, is simply not a good idea. Maybe you've been hanging out with him over a few days or weeks, but remember that you are seeing him out of his own context. As far as you are concerned, he has no history except for what he has told you, which could easily be a fabrication.

## HOW INDIANS SEE US

The Indian media tends to portray foreign women as promiscuous, and this is the predominant impression most Indians have. For many Indian men, especially those of the uneducated classes, what they see on the screen is all they know about us. As a result, some men think it's OK to treat foreign women like prostitutes, especially when their dress and demeanor are indecent by local standards. The fact that some women do come to India looking for sex contributes to the impression that we are all like that.

It doesn't help that many Bollywood movies portray women as sex objects. Storylines often have the hero teasing and harassing his leading lady until she marries him and they live happily ever after. It gives some men the idea that this is the way girls secretly want to be treated—and that this is the way women *should* be treated.

When women from less conservative countries dress and act as if they were back home, they often don't realize that they are doing anything inappropriate. But remember that even in cosmopolitan settings where it appears that "everyone" is dressing or acting in ways that don't reflect the values of the much more conservative majority, there are always people in the background who are likely to get turned on or offended by behaviors and manners of dress that wouldn't be considered provocative back home.

One thing you simply must accept is that you will inevitably get stared at a lot, by women as well as men. Staring isn't necessarily harassment. It's just that Indians are curious about us and want to understand how our lives are different from theirs. But staring back at men could be misinterpreted as an invitation, so just look away.

Fair skin is highly prized in India, and Indian men are often strongly attracted to women with light coloring. If you are fair, especially if you are blond, you will often find people taking your photo, either openly or secretly. You'll start to feel like a celebrity with all the attention.

In certain ways, a light complexion can be an advantage. Even though we don't really fit into the Indian social structure, Westerners in general and Caucasians in particular are almost universally believed to be rich and therefore, by inference, powerful, which gives us a certain status. The risk of rape is likely to be less on account of that status.

It seems to be commonly understood that messing with a foreigner is particularly risky and could bring severe consequences.

## ESSENTIALS OF PREVENTION

Mental preparation is the most important aspect of prevention. Cultivate the right attitude and demeanor; make a habit of being alert and in the present; understand and respect the culture; and always know where you are.

Act confident even if you don't feel it. Your attitude and how you carry yourself has everything to do with how people treat you. It's essential to project an image of someone who deserves respect and can take care of herself. An appearance of confidence and purposefulness is enough to deflect much potential harassment. Stand tall and hold your head high.

Be confidently cool and aloof with men you don't know. When you are passing men on the street, especially groups, give a brief, uninterested, even dismissive, glance, and then immediately look away with an air of indifference. If they know that you are aware of their presence, they aren't likely to try to sneak up on you.

Smile at the world, but don't direct friendly looks to strange men, as they might think it's a come-on.

Avoid looking men in the eye, even in passing, as this can be seen as an indication that you are out looking for sex.

Trust your intuition. Sometimes there may be nothing that is obviously 'wrong' with a situation or a person, but if your gut feeling is that something doesn't feel right, always go with your feelings and get out. Leave at the first feeling of danger. Don't wait to see what happens.

Be alert to what's going on around you, especially when you are out and about. Don't go around listening to music or talking on the phone. Keep your awareness in the present. Whenever you need to text or talk on your cell phone, find a safe place to sit down and do it. Always be aware of your surroundings.

Print out or write down contact details and directions wherever you are headed. Don't depend on having Internet access.

Always know where you are. Get local maps or download them on your smartphone—and use them. Do carry a map when you are in a strange city, but don't stand around on the street trying to figure out where you are. Go into a store or cafe to read it. Moving around without paying attention to your surroundings makes you an easy target for thieves, predators and gropers—not to mention that it puts you at risk from careless drivers.

If you stop to take a selfie, look around before you do and don't let it take your awareness away from your surroundings. Getting absorbed in the process of taking a selfie, as so many people do makes you exceptionally vulnerable.

Make a habit of noticing the people around you wherever you go. If you see anyone or anything that doesn't feel right, pay more attention and move away.

Never accept food or drink from strangers, especially on trains or buses or around major tourist sites. Instances of travelers being drugged and robbed are not unknown. When people offer, it is best to thank them, while politely and firmly declining. A smile and simple hand gesture are usually sufficient. Most people understand and are not offended. However, if someone has ill intentions, he or she may pretend to feel hurt by your refusal and your lack of trust. This is just an act. You're not declining their hospitality while at their own house, and you certainly have no obligation to trust someone you just met, even if you have been sitting together for several hours. Even if they offer something that appears unopened, or if they take a cookie from a package before offering some to you, politely decline.

Incidentally, taking tea in a reputable shop is generally quite safe, especially if there are other customers. If you have any doubt, decline. The surest way to decline hospitality without offending anyone is to say, "I'm fasting just now." Maybe you will break your fast as soon as you are out of their sight, but they don't need to know that. Fasting is understood all over India as it is common for people to fast both for religious and health reasons. Ignore beggars and touts; they will keep following you and harassing you if you show even the slightest interest in them. Also, if you give anything to one beggar, you are likely to be surrounded by many more and that can get scary. Never go anywhere with a tout.

Be evasive and avoid answering overly personal questions. If you are alone, avoid saying so. Some people recommend wearing a wedding band, and maybe carrying a photo of your "husband", as well. Although it can be a useful ploy in certain circumstances, I really don't recommend it. Lying leads to all sorts of complications. Truthful evasions are better. However, if you choose to pretend you are married, think out your story in advance so you don't embarrass yourself. You will inevitably be bombarded with questions like, "Where is he? What does he do? Why isn't he with you? When is he coming? What about your children?"

Personally, I often just say that I'm never alone and leave it at that. It's truthful from my perspective, though I don't bother to explain what I mean. Sometimes I just vaguely say that my friends are 'around', without specifying where. Another evasive strategy that I use a lot is to turn the tables and ask the questioner about himself. It's a good distraction because most people love to talk about themselves.

Find out as much as you can about a place even before you go there. Check the local news occasionally to find out if there is some big demonstration or festival planned, or anything you might need to know about. Knowledge is always empowering, so the more you have, the better.

Don't walk alone at night, and avoid walking alone in isolated or bad areas even in the daytime. If you aren't comfortable with the area, carry some pepper spray in a way that you can use it quickly if need be. You can buy it in all major cities in India. You'll probably never need it, but having it at hand does add a feeling of security.

You are much more likely to need pepper spray for monkeys and mad dogs than men, but it can be a lifesaver if you find yourself in a sticky situation somewhere. Packs of street dogs can be dangerous, especially at night, so stay away from them.

Although prevention is the most important thing, it's good to learn some self-defense tactics to gain confidence in knowing how to deal with men who misbehave. Considering the amount of violence against women in the world today, every woman should know at least a little basic self-defense no matter where she is. If you don't have time to take classes, at least watch a few self-defense videos. There are plenty of good ones on YouTube.

Don't wear expensive clothes, jewelry or other accessories except for specific occasions where it's appropriate. Even then, tone it down. Looking wealthy can attract too much of the wrong sort of attention.

Keep your passport, money, credit cards, etc. in an inner pocket or money pouch, but be sure you can access them easily and modestly. Always carry enough cash to get back to where you are staying, and then some. Don't keep all your money in one place.

Avoid using ATMs at night. The ones inside banks are the safest, if you can find one.

Carry a flashlight at night. Power outages are a frequent occurrence all over India, and you don't want to be caught outside without a light. A small keychain flashlight is convenient because you can keep it with you all the time, so if you are out unexpectedly late, you at least have that much light.

You may have lots of people asking to take a photo with you, even if you have never seen them before. If it's a group of boys, they may be just looking for an excuse to put their arms around you; and you may end up getting groped or pinched. It's OK to say 'no'.

Probably the biggest risk to personal safety in India is the traffic rather than people, so pay attention to it whenever you are on the street.

You also have to be careful of monkeys and street dogs. Monkeys will try to steal anything you are carrying, but they also bite. If you get bitten by either a dog or any other animal, go immediately to the nearest hospital for rabies shots. If a monkey steals something, they will drop it if you throw some food for them — they have an excellent understanding of ransom!

Avoid the drug scene. Drugs and safety simply do not go together. Places known for drug abuse and rave parties, including parts of Goa, are said to have many rapes that don't get reported. This may be in part because the victims are afraid of going to jail for drug-related crimes, as the penalties can be extreme. The fact that a girl has been raped while stoned might not be protection from being prosecuted for the drugs.

Never let anyone ridicule or manipulate you into abandoning your good security habits. Trust your own feelings about what you need to do to feel safe.

## SAFE INTERACTIONS WITH INDIAN MEN

If a man is misinterpreting your intentions, let him know it immediately. Get away from men who ignore your personal space and try to cozy up to you when you haven't invited it.

Learn to be reserved with men, while at the same time radiating a confident feeling of universal friendliness. This attitude is a much better protection than being wary and tense, which can attract the wrong kind of attention because it makes you look weak and vulnerable. This may take a bit of cultivation, but the rewards are worth it. It is said that the world is as you are, so this means that radiating friendliness to everyone around you will tend to make the people you meet and your environment friendlier towards you.

India is not a country where flirting and wearing sexy clothes is a normal part of the culture and of the way men and women relate to each other. Dressing and acting in a way that is designed to be as sexually attractive to men as possible is unintentionally inviting trouble. If you dress or act in a sexually provocative manner, don't be surprised if men try to grope you, etc. You'll be regarded as fair game.

Don't flirt with a man unless you want to end up in bed with him. Flirting is not usually taken as innocent fun in India. It's seen as a definite invitation for sex. Even casual conversations with men you meet in passing, such as on a train, may be misinterpreted and lead to unwanted sexual advances. Be reserved in such situations and avoid answering personal questions about yourself. If the conversation turns to sex, shut him out and leave.

If a man is intent on rape, he will usually try to get you alone. If you accept anyone's offer to show you the way somewhere, be alert. Don't follow blindly or go where there's no one around or where there are only men.

Avoid situations where you will be alone with an Indian man. Your willingness to be alone with a man even in an innocent situation may be misinterpreted as an invitation for greater intimacy.

Do not allow men to come into your room, or go into theirs unless that's what you want. If you have to have a repairman come, try to have someone else there with you, or at least leave the door open while he is there.

While a head massage in a busy salon is OK, a full-body massage by a man in a private room definitely isn't. Whether or not he behaves honorably, it is bound to give others the wrong ideas. Always insist on having a woman do the massage.

Even in offices and other professional situations, be careful about being alone with a man. Unfortunately, it's necessary to be alert for indications that men are getting unwelcome ideas even in situations where you wouldn't expect it.

Don't accept unsolicited help from men who come up and offer to show you around, help you find something, etc. Just ignore them and keep moving.

It's usually OK to ask men for directions if there are no women to ask, etc., but be discriminating about who you approach for information. Avoid approaching beggars, laborers, touts, groups of men, or rough-looking people. It's much better to go into decent shops or restaurants if there is no one on the street you feel comfortable talking to.

## CONNECTING FOR SAFETY

Stay connected. Keep people informed of your whereabouts. If you have a pre-planned itinerary, send it to friends or family members and try to include telephone numbers where you can be reached. Be in touch with someone regularly. If you are planning something risky, let someone know the details.

Don't hesitate to approach and make friends with local women. A big smile is often enough to break the ice. Ask them about local customs and the safest ways of doing things. If you are being harassed, do reach out to any women who may be around.

Whenever you go out at night, tell someone where you are going and when you expect to be back. Avoid staying out late unless you are with someone you know and trust.

Smartphones are a great asset when it comes to personal safety. However, they do pose a significant health hazard, so you have to decide for yourself whether the tradeoff is worth it. If you have one, take the time to program all your important contact numbers into it, and be familiar with emergency numbers wherever you are. There will soon be a national emergency number like 911 in the US, but as of now it hasn't happened. It is said that the number will be 112. Check out the great free women's safety apps that are available for India.

Get in the habit of sending photos of people you are hanging out or traveling with. Do it in the spirit of fun rather than making it a chore, but be aware that this habit could be a lifesaver if you run into problems. With a smartphone or a camera with an Indian SIM and a data plan, you can send photos as soon as you take them.

In case you are alone and feeling unsafe—if, for instance, someone is following you or watching you with too much interest—don't be afraid to ask other women or families if you can tag along with them. Indians will almost always welcome you, and you may end up making new friends while you are at it. If language barriers prevent an explanation, just stay near them anyway.

## THE NEED FOR RESPECT

Many women unknowingly make themselves a target of unnecessary harassment simply because they don't understand the culture. Learning how to avoid major cultural blunders will go a long way towards keeping you safe.

Fortunately, most Indians don't expect visitors from other countries to be perfectly tuned in to the nuances of the local culture, but if you do your best to be respectful, people will notice, and you will be treated with greater respect, as well. Respecting the standards of the local culture can greatly reduce the risk of sexual harassment.

If you dress and behave in a way that is sufficiently modest to honor the local standards, you won't stand out in a bad way. It's important to get into the habit of dressing, speaking and behaving much more modestly than you would at home. The way you dress and behave has a significant influence on how successfully you interact with the locals and how they perceive you.

Smoking, drinking, using drugs and swearing are habits that are generally regarded as being indications of a loose moral character in women almost everywhere in the country. Strong profanity is regarded as disrespectful, so if you are in the habit of swearing a lot, try to tone down your language. Doing these things in public just reinforces the negative stereotype people have of foreign women.

If you behave intimately with your partner in public (hugging, kissing, or fondling each other), you may be unwittingly sending a message to passersby that you are a sex-starved woman who may be available to anyone, even if you have no eyes for anyone else. So save your intimacies—as well as your sexy clothes and flirtatious behavior—for when you are alone together.

It's easy to get confused about what's appropriate in any given place because rather than a single, homogeneous culture that pervades the whole country, there are more than a hundred distinct cultures, many of which have little in common with each other.

Nevertheless, India's many cultures and subcultures are generally conservative, and women are expected to dress and act modestly. Unfortunately, quite a few people have the idea that cultural requirements of modesty are a justification for victim-blaming, but that is a narrow, over-simplified view that doesn't take other important factors into account.

Many cultures have conservative standards of dress and behavior that have evolved over countless generations, and the reasons behind them are complex. To assume, for instance, that traditional women's clothing is only about modesty and about blaming women for men's sexual misconduct is a mistake. Traditional dress is an essential aspect of cultural identity, which is something that should be preserved. It would be tragic for India to lose its cultural diversity, which is one of the things that make it so wonderful.

Westerners are often critical of certain aspects of Indian society, not all of which are necessarily deserving of criticism. Some people assume, for instance, that all Indian women are oppressed and long to behave and dress as Westerners do. While that may apply to some women, it certainly doesn't apply to all. India is not an individualistic society, and there is no reason why it must become one. Western standards are suitable for the West, not for India. When outsiders who don't understand a society and the value of its customs attempt to impose change because they think only their values are valid, it creates more problems.

As Alvaro Enterria so aptly put it: "Consciously or unconsciously, the idea that Western values are the universally valid human values prevails in the West. But to attempt to use our parameters and ways of thinking to judge or attempt to understand a society and culture that, being based on very different principles, eludes our grasp, is to run the serious risk of not understanding anything."[4]

---

[4] Alvaro Enterria, India From Within, Indica Books, Varanasi, 2010, p.18

In order to even begin to understand Indian society, it's necessary to understand the concept of *izzat*, which is fundamental to social interactions in India. *Izzat* is one's honor, as well as one's self-respect, one's self-esteem. Moreover, there is also a collective *izzat* that belongs to families, clans, castes, the various Indian cultures, tribes, religious groups, political parties, and, of course, the nation as a whole. How much respect is given to a person or group is determined by strict but unwritten hierarchical rules, which every Indian learns from infancy. These rules govern all aspects of behavior in India, and how individuals and groups relate to each other.

If one should fail to give the respect that a person feels is due to himself, his religion, his family, etc., it can "... provoke an irrational response totally disproportionate to the level of the slight."[5] Fortunately, most Indians are pretty tolerant and forgiving of ignorant mistakes and even bad behavior on the part of visitors.

When visitors go around flagrantly disrespecting cultural norms, either out of ignorance or prejudice, or because they simply don't care, or even have the misguided idea that they are somehow helping to 'liberate' Indian women, they are insulting the

---

[5] Pavan K. Varma, *Being Indian,* Penguin Books, New Delhi, 2004, pp. 39–40.

collective honor. Whether they realize it or not, they are also undermining their own honor and showing themselves to be undeserving of respect. They offend many people and attract unnecessary harassment. This kind of behavior also reflects poorly on the collective honor of the visitors' own country.

## THE BASIC INDIAN DRESS CODE

How you dress profoundly affects how people respond to you, and this is even more the case in India than in most other countries.

Although we shouldn't have to worry about men getting the wrong idea because of our clothes, the practical reality is that honoring local standards of dress definitely helps. Unfortunately, as foreigners, we are already at a disadvantage due to common misconceptions, so it is safer to dress conservatively.

Girls who dress and act modestly are more highly regarded than those who flout the cultural norms, and they are safer from sexual harassment. If you dress immodestly according to local standards, some people will inevitably treat you like a prostitute.

In spite of the differences from place to place, there is a kind of basic Indian dress code, and it's vital to understand it, and the reasons behind it because it's an essential part of projecting an image of someone who deserves respect. Basic standards of modesty almost everywhere require that you cover your knees, upper arms, shoulders, cleavage and midriff, though the standards are even more conservative in many areas. Tops should not show your cleavage or be too tight or revealing. Leave your sheer blouses, shorts, spaghetti-strap dresses, bikinis, tank tops, etc. at home. Wearing clothing that is indecent by local standards is insulting to the culture. It also gives men the idea that you are "available"—even if your behavior clearly indicates the opposite.

While researching this book, I spoke with many women about their experiences with Indian men. Those who did not respect the Indian standards of dress almost invariably reported far more problems with harassment.

For the vast majority of Indians, the basic standards of modesty are compulsory. It's true that many girls and women—especially in major tourist places like Mumbai, Delhi, and Goa—tend to dress in ways that are considered immodest by most traditional standards, but they are definitely not in the majority in most of the country. Times are changing, but for now, this is still the reality.

Indian men generally prefer to see modestly dressed women, both because such attire shows respect for the culture, and because it doesn't put unnecessary strain on their self-control. Most Indians, including women, are embarrassed to see women wearing skimpy clothes. To my surprise, on two or three occasions men have come up to me on the street and thanked me for dressing modestly and respecting their culture! This was, as you might expect, in an area where many female tourists dress inappropriately by local standards—and some even by most Western standards.

If you are in a cosmopolitan environment where you have little direct contact with traditional Indians, you may feel that you can safely wear whatever you please, but I would still advise you to dress fairly conservatively.

In order to make yourself less of a target, it is advisable to avoid looking like a tourist, even if you are one. This is something that experts recommend for travel almost everywhere, and it is certainly important in India. It's not about trying to disguise the fact that you are a foreigner. Most of us couldn't do so, anyway. But save the souvenir clothes such as the Taj Mahal T-shirts for when you get home.

In spite of their great popularity, it's also better to avoid the cheap, hippyish clothes made for tourists that Indians seldom wear. They mark you as a tourist just as clearly as the Taj Mahal T-shirts do.

Yoga wear—except for loose *kurta pajamas*—does not qualify as street clothes in India. Save it for the yoga studio or your room.

Nevertheless, what kind of clothes you choose to wear is not nearly as important as how you wear them. Since standards vary from place to place, you can look around at how most of the local women dress (*not* other tourists), and cover up to a similar extent. If you don't want to always have to think about what to wear, you can just follow the general guidelines below to feel comfortable almost anywhere in India.

Though sleeveless tops are fairly common in some places during the hot season, in most places they are not acceptable. It's better to at least cover your upper arms. While you might think it would make you feel too hot, being fully covered with loose, lightweight (but not transparent!) cotton clothes can actually be cooler and more comfortable than going around with bare arms and legs. The Indian sun can be brutal.

It's acceptable for your midriff to be exposed when wearing a sari, but not otherwise. Shorts and short skirts are generally not acceptable. A bra is essential unless you are as flat-chested as a child, but underwear should not show at all.

While it's generally acceptable to wear Western clothes, it's essential to wear them in a manner that is respectful to the culture. However, there are some exceptionally conservative places where it may be better to wear traditional Indian clothes. There are also a few temples where ladies will not be admitted unless they are wearing a sari, though Western clothes are acceptable in most temples as long as they are modest.

When wearing pants, loose, tunic-style tops that cover your buttocks and crotch are best. A long, not-too-tight T-shirt also works. Though many of us like to wear our tops neatly tucked in, here it's better to let them hang out. It's also cooler in the hot weather.

Your swimsuit should be a conservative one, no matter where you plan to wear it. Although there are certain beaches, especially in Goa, where it seems that "everyone" wears bikinis, I'd advise against it. In any case, on the way to or from the beach or pool, or whenever you are interacting with locals, put on something modest over your swimsuit. Incidentally, swimming or sunbathing alone on a remote beach is not a good idea, no matter what you are wearing.

Public nudity is unacceptable everywhere (*naga babas* and small children not with standing), and a swimsuit or other clothes must be worn even when bathing in a remote location. Underwear is absolutely not acceptable bathing attire for women, though men can get away with it. Oh, that double standard again!

If you have long (below shoulder-length) hair, it's best to wear it tied back or up in some way. Leaving it loose can be seen as immodest.

## ALL ABOUT INDIAN CLOTHES...

Girls who wear traditional Indian clothes generally report that they receive more respect than when they wear Western dress. It also serves as a great icebreaker. Many people will comment on it, and you will find that the comments are almost always positive because it shows your appreciation of their culture.

Incidentally, well-cut Indian suits and well-draped saris flatter just about every figure—much better than most Western clothes—not to mention the fact that they are incredibly comfortable when made of natural fabrics. Really lightweight cottons are especially well-suited to the climate.

There are several varieties of ladies' pantsuits: the *salwar-kameez* (a.k.a. Punjabi suit), which consists of a long tunic top *(kameez)* over baggy pants *(salwar)* which are banded at the bottom; or the *churidhar-kameez,* which has the *kameez* over skinny straight pants *(churidhar)* that are worn bunched around the calf and ankle. Another popular style is the *anarkali* dress, which can be worn with either a *salwar* or *churidhar*. Incidentally, *churidhars* and *anarkali* dresses are mainly worn by younger women and teens, and not so much by older women. A scarf *(chunni* or *dupatta)* draped across the front completes the outfit. It's an essential part of the ensemble, so don't leave it off. You can buy suits readymade or else you can buy a "suit piece", which consists of three coordinated pieces of fabric (for the top, pants and scarf), and have it made up by a tailor.

For a more international look, get the pants made with a straight leg; or else buy readymade tops *(kurtas)* to wear over your Western-style pants. This look is more flexible in terms of the scarf. You can wear it however you like or even dispense with it altogether without making the outfit look all wrong. However, it's good to carry a scarf or shawl no matter what you are wearing in case you need it to protect your face from dust, or if you wish to go into a temple, etc. And in conservative places, it's good to wear it anyway to honor the local standards of modesty.

The *sari,* which is arguably the most beautiful style of dress in the world, is the most common form of women's clothing. It's worn almost everywhere in India, although it's wrapped in different ways according to local custom. If you are going to a wedding or special celebration or a temple, it's almost always appropriate. On the other hand, there are places where you might find that you attract too much attention wearing a *sari,* such as on the streets of Delhi or Mumbai.

*Saris* can be both modest and sexy, depending on the blouse and style of wearing the *sari,* but don't go to the extreme of wearing blouses that are too skimpy. Wearing your *sari* too low on your hips, whether for a sexier look or because you are especially tall, is also not acceptable. *Saris* should be worn long so that the bottom is no more than about an inch or two off the ground with your shoes on; your ankles are not supposed to show. If you are tall, you may need to have an extra piece of matching fabric added to the part you tuck in. It won't show, and the sari will look much better than if you wear it badly.

Incidentally, *sari* petticoats may look like long drawstring skirts, but they are only meant to be worn under saris. They are made of plain cotton, usually with a ruffle at the bottom. The fitted, midriff-revealing blouse (*choli*) that you wear under a *sari,* is also only intended for wearing with a *sari.* Wearing it with jeans, etc. is not acceptable.

One thing that can up the respect factor is to get your clothes neatly pressed. In most places there are press-walas who will iron your clothes for a few rupees, and it's worth taking advantage of their services whenever you can. A person who is well-dressed is more highly regarded than someone whose appearance is sloppy or dirty. If you go around looking grubby, you won't get much respect. Avoid clothes that the locals think of as being appropriate for lower classes even if you think they look cool. Do your best to be neat and clean at all times. If you don't have time to wash your clothes, you are moving too fast.

It's impossible to overstate the value of respect in how you are treated in India—and it goes both ways. Respect is something you must also give. As well as showing that you are deserving of respect, dressing well is seen in the Indian culture as something that shows respect. Look around and you will see that almost all women make the effort to look as good as they can in their circumstances. Diane Sharma Winter expresses it well: "Indians totally appreciate a well turned out woman and usually treat you differently once you have passed their initial assessment. In most situations Indians assess the character of a person by the cut of their cloth, instantly and instinctively. This is not so much snobbish as it is cultural in origin. Traditionally in India, caste and position were immediately obvious by the way in which a person dressed. From the placement of jewelry to the length of a turban, the dress code in India is so intricately wedded into the DNA of the average Indian that it's impossible to decode…." [6]

Indians won't usually tell you if you are doing something they consider inappropriate—but they

[6] Diane Sharma Winter http://www.womentravelmotherindia.com/what-to-wear-in-india-the-rule-of-the-three-bs/

will definitely notice. If it's something that has caused them to lose respect for you, they will probably try to hide their lack of respect out of natural politeness or cultural conditioning. Nevertheless, it will still affect how you are received.

The more respect you get, the safer you will be. People tend to respond to you as you present yourself.

## HASSLE-FREE ARRIVAL

Always book your first night in advance even if you plan to be completely spontaneous the rest of the time. If you arrive at night, you should arrange for someone to pick you up at the airport, especially if you are traveling alone. It's wonderfully comforting to have someone standing at the airport exit with your name on a placard when you arrive. Be sure to get the name and mobile number of the driver meeting you so you can call him if necessary. At the airport, you can buy an Indian SIM card valid for 30 days, or call from a public phone booth. Confirm your reservation and your pickup in advance.

At airports, railway stations, and tourist sites, many taxi and auto-rickshaw drivers, touts, and even porters solicit travelers with offers of ridiculously cheap transportation, tours, and hotels. Avoid these offers and avoid touts in general. Aside from putting you in a potentially risky situation, they usually end up being far more expensive than you are led to expect.

If a prearranged ride is not possible, get a prepaid taxi. There are usually a few options, ranging from basic to luxurious. The cheapest ones are usually OK in the daytime, but at night the risk of breakdowns is a more serious matter as these taxis are almost all pretty decrepit. You are also more likely to have problems with the drivers themselves. In general, it's safer to go with a reputable taxi company like EasyCab or Meru Cabs.

When taking a cab from the airport, be sure that the registration number on your slip of paper matches the vehicle; don't give it to the driver until you reach your destination.

Taxi drivers will sometimes say that your hotel is closed for repairs even if you have a confirmed reservation, or else that the road is blocked and you can't get to it, or that the hotel is no good and they know somewhere better. Don't believe it, especially if they tell you that every hotel is booked and they want to take you to another city. Threaten to use the 'panic button', if there is one, or to inform the Traffic Police if they won't cooperate—or get out and take another cab. Never allow yourself to be taken anywhere you don't want to go. If you have to call the hotel from the driver's phone, insist on dialing the number yourself so you know you are really talking to the hotel and aren't being scammed.

# SAFE PLACES TO STAY

Many of the best places to stay come through recommendations from other travelers. But even if a place comes highly recommended, should you feel something is wrong when you get there, look for another place. Trust your feelings.

If possible, do an on-line check of reviews for any accommodation you are considering. If there is a report of inappropriate behavior towards women, look elsewhere. Also check to see if there have been any crimes reported there.

Never go with a tout to look at a room and never book any accommodation through a tout.

If you use a service like Couchsurfing or AirBNB, be careful about staying with single men unless they have several positive reviews from other girls. Some guys seem to think that if a girl is willing to stay at their place, they are up for sharing their bed, but that's not how those services are meant to be used. If a host acts inappropriately, report him immediately.

Don't accept hospitality from strangers. For the sake of courtesy, you can thank them and say that you'd love to visit sometime, but don't make a commitment. Even if you have just spent many hours with them on the train and it feels like they are now good friends, you can't really know. If you want to meet up with them later, ask to meet at a restaurant or somewhere in public. If they keep pressing you and won't accept your excuses, don't be afraid to say a firm no. Never let yourself be bullied into going with anyone. You aren't obliged to give in to their agenda.

Indians are wonderfully hospitable people, but some are so eager for visitors that they could be described as aggressively hospitable. You may meet complete strangers in airports or on trains who insist that you must come and stay with them within the first few minutes of your conversation! In such a culture, their motives might actually be pure, but don't count on it.

If you are traveling alone, try not to arrive in a new place without having a room pre-booked, especially if you will be arriving late. Don't depend on a taxi or rickshaw driver to get you a decent hotel. They tend to be more interested in the commission they will receive for taking you there than your welfare.

When you are staying in a hotel, check the windows to make sure they can be closed and locked securely. If the doors and windows are not secure, get a different room. Keep your door locked even when you are in the room. A rubber doorstop is a good extra security measure, especially in budget places, which don't always have good deadbolts.

Don't leave your window open at night unless it has a security screen or is safely away from any potential access.

Whenever you have to answer the door, be sure you are modestly covered, preferably in street clothes. Answering the door in your nightie or bikini or underwear is extremely foolish no matter where you are. If there is a chain or peep-hole, use it before opening the door. If there is an unexpected knock on the door, call the front desk to verify who it is.

When signing a hotel register, use only your initials without a title that gives away your gender (i.e., Ms., Miss or Mrs.)

Avoid leave your key lying around where someone could see your room number, which you don't want advertised.

Ask to have your room cleaned only when you are there. It's best not to leave a "Please Clean My Room" sign on the door when you are out.

Always get a business card or piece of paper with the address and phone number and name of your host, or someone where you are staying, and keep it with you whenever you go out. You may want to get it written out in the local language, too. And you really don't want to venture out and suddenly realize that you don't know how to get back.

Avoid staying alone on houseboats, especially in isolated situations. Always get recommendations for safe houseboats and ask what the deal is in advance. Never book through a tout.

It's not safe to camp by yourself. Even in an extremely remote area, you can never be certain that someone has not observed where you have gone to camp. In some areas, it's not safe to camp even in a group. Ask the locals about the situation before pitching your tent.

While your belongings are obviously much less important than your personal security, losing your passport and money could put you at any sort of risk.

No matter where you are staying, you don't want to leave your valuables in an unlocked bag. Just keep it locked all the time. If your host says, "Oh, that's not necessary here", tell them you appreciate that, but because you won't always be somewhere so safe, you simply can't afford to get out of the habit. If they don't respect that, you might be inclined to wonder whether it really is so safe there.

## SAFETY ON THE MOVE

Of the various categories of taxis, the safest are taxis driven by women, radio taxis from reliable companies, and taxis that you get from a five-star hotel (which you can do even if you aren't staying there) rather than the ones you flag down on the road or find at general taxi stands. The radio cabs often have safety features such as on-board GPS systems, which others don't. You can book them online or over the phone. When they confirm, they will send you a text message with the driver's name and cell number. The driver calls you when he reaches the pickup place so you don't have to wait around outside.

If you have hired a car for the day, always get the driver's name, cell phone number and car number. If he has to move the car while you are gone, or there is a problem, you will be able to find him. You can call the driver to pick you up right at the door if he is parked some distance away. Late at night you should always do this.

Always write the name and address of your destination on a piece of paper—one you don't need to get back. Do your best to know where you are going. Carry a map and hold it like you know the area. You can also use your GPS on your phone.

The driver may want to bring a friend or relative along, or pick up someone along the way, but don't let him get away with it, especially if you are alone or it's after dark. It's not uncommon for taxi drivers to give false excuses for taking on other passengers at your expense; and you just never know who they are. On the other hand, policemen often flag down taxis for a free ride, and there's nothing you can do about it.

If your driver suddenly stops on a dark, deserted road for no apparent reason, tell him in no uncertain terms to keep moving. If he seems to have bad intentions and you feel threatened, get out the pepper spray and your mobile, if you have them. In case there is a mechanical problem or flat tire, stay in car with the doors locked while he deals with it.

Whenever you are riding in a car, keep the doors locked, especially at night. Roll the windows up if you stop at a light where there are beggars or itinerant vendors (unless you actually want to buy something), or guys on motorbikes taking too much interest in you.

If you can afford it, consider hiring a car and driver for the duration of your trip. You'll always have someone with you who is motivated to keep you safe. And a good driver can really make for a pleasant journey. Never pay the whole amount in advance in order to keep him motivated.

You can often flag down taxis, auto-rickshaws and jeeps on the road even if they have other passengers. You can usually tell by the license plates and the color of the vehicle whether it is for hire, though this is something that differs from place to place, so you'll have to ask someone. However, it is not advisable to do this unless there are other women or families in the car. You can also find shared jeeps and taxis in the hills and rural areas at certain taxi stands. If you want more space, ask for the whole front seat. It's almost always worth the extra rupees.

Many travel agents will arrange shared taxis to distant destinations. Try to use an agent who is known to you or your friends, if possible, or who is well-recommended. Let someone know your travel plans, as well as the agent's contact information, the car number and driver's name.

Hitchhiking is not recommended. But if for some reason you need to get a ride with strangers, be discriminating about whom you accept a ride with. Don't just hop in blithely without looking carefully at the driver and other occupants as well as the vehicle's state of decrepitude. If you have a bad feeling, don't get in, especially if they insist. Don't get in a car with a bunch of men, even if it is the only ride around. Even two is too many if you are a woman alone.

Don't take rides from strangers at night. If you are stuck somewhere, it's almost always better to find a safe place to stay until morning rather than trying to move on. Let someone know where you are and what the situation is, even if they are far away.

Whenever you take a ride with someone you don't know, whether in a private car or on a motorbike—or even a taxi, especially at night or if you are even slightly doubtful about the situation—get the license number and driver's name, then call or text it to someone. Let them know where you are going and when you expect to arrive. If you can't reach anyone, then at least pretend you have, loudly repeating the information so the driver can hear. Or make sure someone where you are getting in knows who you are going with. Tell them you will call when you arrive.

Never sit next to the driver in an auto-rickshaw; there's no way to avoid being too close. It's good to keep pepper spray handy when riding alone in an auto-rickshaw, especially at night.

Go for the ladies' queue for train and bus tickets, if there is one. Sometimes women can just go to the head of the queue if there isn't a special one. If you get sandwiched between men in a mixed queue, don't hesitate to tell them to give you more space. Hold your bag in front of you, and give a gentle hint with your elbows if you have to. Indians tend to crush together whenever they get in a queue, even if there is plenty of room.

When traveling alone by train, First AC is an excellent option if you can afford it. It's the most secure and you are unlikely to have problems. The compartments are lockable, and there are attendants in the car that you can call in case of need. I've never experienced even the slightest harassment in First AC.

There is considerable debate on whether it's safe for a single woman to travel overnight in Sleeper Class. I don't recommend it. True, you are surrounded by lots of people, which will usually avert any serious problems, but I'd advise finding someone to travel with anyway or going for a higher class. At least, try to make sure you are in with families or couples. You can ask the TTE (conductor) to move you if you feel uncomfortable; or you can ask around for someone to trade berths. Get an upper berth, if possible, to make it harder for potential molesters to get at you or for voyeurs to snap photos of you sleeping.

While violent assault on trains is rare, harassment of some sort is not, especially in the lower classes of travel. Even if you are with a man, you might suffer harassment, especially if you don't take care to respect the culture. Avoiding physical contact is particularly important.

If you travel alone in Unreserved Class, you may want to go for the Ladies' Compartment.

For overnight journeys, wear something modest and comfortable, such as a salwar-kameez or a kurta-pajama set—Indian street clothes that are as comfortable as pyjamas. Cover up well when you are sleeping.

Trains heading for holy places typically have more families on board than trains between business centers, which often have a predominance of men.

The Delhi Metro has a woman's compartment where you can escape the crush. There's one car on every train, and it is almost always the least crowded.

Avoid taking public transportation at night—particularly night buses and overnight buses—especially if you are traveling alone. If you take an overnight bus, go for the super deluxe option, if available. It's worth the few extra rupees. Sleeper buses have two berths on one side and one on the other. If you are alone, go for the singles. Semi-sleeper buses are two by two, so you don't have that option. Absolutely avoid any bus at night that only has men on it or that is empty of passengers. Don't get on even if you have already paid for the ticket.

Some buses have a women's section, usually at the front. If you are alone, try to sit next to other women. On crowded buses, window seats are better than the aisle, as you won't have people hanging over you. Since local buses often have people packed in like sardines, a window seat is the only place where you have any breathing room. However, on uncrowded buses, the aisle is better as it's easier to move if some creepy guy sits down next to you. You can always shift to the window seat if another woman comes along. If a local bus is too crowded, wait for a less crowded one or else opt for a private taxi or autorickshaw—or even walk, if it's not too far.

In waiting rooms, it's safest to sit near women and families rather than off by yourself. Some stations have ladies' waiting rooms, so go for those if they are available.

Avoid packing more than you can manage on your own. It's better to be mobile and not dependent on others more than necessary. If you have to struggle with your bags, you make yourself an easy target in more ways than one.

Walk or jog facing the traffic, but do be aware of traffic coming up behind you. Indians don't always bother about being on the right side of the street.

Wearing dark glasses when you are out walking around allows you to look at everyone around you without them seeing. It also helps to deflect some harassment. But do take your sunglasses off when you are engaged in conversation, even if it's just to ask directions. A wide-brim hat is also useful for hiding from unwanted stares.

It's good to wear comfortable shoes when you are out and about, so you can move quickly if need be.

## SETTLING IN FOR A LONGER STAY

Before you choose a place to stay, check the neighborhood out thoroughly. Ask the neighbors how safe the area is and if there is anything you need to be aware of.

Once you move in, take some time to get familiar with the neighborhood. Walk around learning where everything is, including the local police station and hospital.

Go out of your way to make friends with local women and families in your neighborhood, and don't hesitate to ask them for advice. It's safer not to be a total stranger. If they are shy, just keep smiling and saying 'hello'; eventually, they should warm up to you.

Learn a few words of the local language wherever you are, unless you are on a whirlwind tour. Include a few emergency expressions such as "help me". Aside from the fact that you won't be totally helpless if you have to communicate with people who don't speak English, you'll find that people you meet tend to be friendlier if you make even a tiny effort to learn their language.

When you are staying in a place for some time, don't get into a set routine, such as jogging the same route at the same time every day. Vary the time and route each day.

If you hire local people, get them verified by the police before they start working for you. It's best to hire people with solid references. Find out where they live. Get copies of their identity papers, and take photos.

Don't be casual about it and don't put it off even for a day.

Be careful of people who work for you, especially in your home. Don't put temptation in their way. Being able to hire people to work for you means you are far wealthier than they can even dream of being, so don't flaunt your wealth.

## PRIVACY IS A FOREIGN CONCEPT

Privacy is not always easy to come by in India. Most people don't consider it essential or even desirable except in certain situations.

If you don't keep your door locked—even in your own house—people are likely to come wandering in at just about any time. Friends and servants may walk into your room at any time without knocking. Don't leave your hotel room unlocked, or the staff will assume that they can knock and immediately barge right in without waiting for a response.

If you insist on privacy, people may wonder what you have to hide, and they may take offense sometimes, especially if they are not used to foreigners, because their expectation is that friends have nothing to hide from each other. You may have to explain that customs in your country are different and you need more privacy to feel comfortable and safe. This is really only an issue if you are staying with a family.

## SEX IN INDIAN CULTURE

Most Indians are extremely conservative when it comes to sex. Sexual matters are considered private and are rarely discussed openly. Also, men and women don't mix as freely as in Western countries. Men are expected to keep a respectful distance from women they are not married to. Traditionally, they are even expected to refrain from any physical contact with their wives in public, however slight.

For a man to touch a woman in public, regardless of the intention behind it, is offensive to many people. Physical contact with a person of the opposite sex is a cultural taboo that should be respected when you are in public. Avoid greeting members of the opposite sex in public with hugs and kisses. Even holding hands is not acceptable in most places. In some places you can even be arrested for kissing in public![7]

[7] Mira Kamdar tells in *Planet India* (p. 41) of a couple who was arrested and fined "in lieu of serving a ten-day jail sentence in Rajasthan for kissing each other during their wedding ceremony. . . ."

If you are used to casually touching people when you talk to them, get out of the habit in India, especially when you are speaking to someone of the opposite sex. Even shaking hands with someone of the opposite sex should mostly be avoided, except in international corporate settings. If an Indian man wants to shake your hand, you can usually just *namaskar*[8] instead.

In the West, if a man wants to protect a woman, he may put his arm around her or hold her hand to send a message to other men to leave her alone. In India, it can give the impression that she is a loose woman and fair game for any man.

If you are with a man, ask him to refrain from touching you in public. By treating you in a way that Indians see as respectful, he is signaling that you are a person deserving of respect. Refrain from even looking at each other in an overly intimate way in public. Even though some Indians may behave more intimately in public, it is a bad idea to do likewise.

Indians often hold hands with people of the same sex as a matter of friendship. This is not an indicator of homosexuality. If a woman takes your hand or puts

---

[8] *Namaste* or *namaskar* is spoken with a slight bow and hands pressed together, palms touching and fingers pointing upwards, at about heart level. It may also be spoken without the gesture or performed wordlessly.

her arm around you and it makes you uncomfortable, try to refrain from squirming. Just accept her action as the gesture of friendship it is meant to be, assuming there is nothing inappropriate in the touch.

Homosexuality is still illegal in India, and it's not well-accepted, so if you are gay, it is safer to keep your preferences private.

Once in a while, someone may ask you about your sex life, e.g. how many people you have slept with, etc. No matter what the reality is, look shocked and refuse to answer. You might even slap him hard, if it seems warranted. Questions about your sex life are highly insulting, and most Indians are not so rude. You'll generally get questions like this only from young men whose hormones are raging out of control and who are desperately looking for an outlet. A positive answer—or maybe any answer—will lead them to believe they have found one, and that's likely to be an invitation to trouble of one sort or another. End the conversation and leave.

## DEFLECTING HARASSMENT

Sexual harassment is known by the euphemism, "eve-teasing." Eve-teasing, which includes everything from verbal harassment to any physical molestation short of rape, is a crime, though it's one that the culprits are hardly ever booked for.

Eve-teasing is more common in big cities and tourist towns in the North, especially during festivals such as Holi. Women typically are not seen during street festivals, which inevitably inspire men to get drunk and, consequently, more inclined to sexually aggressive behavior.

There is really no one right way to respond to harassment. It all depends on the situation. You always have to use your best judgment, based on your surroundings, other people present and escape options.

If a man's behavior is inappropriate but doesn't seem dangerous, usually the best thing is to avoid eye contact, maintain silence and get away from him. Don't give him the satisfaction of a response. Any engagement or show of emotion may encourage him, no matter what you say, because that's what he's looking for. No response is no fun for him. And retaliating could easily escalate the situation beyond your control. Staying safe is always the priority.

If you feel threatened, you can use one of the safety apps on your phone that send audio, video and photos to the police and other designated recipients. Or even just pretend you are on your cell phone speaking with the police. It would be good to think this through and practice it in case you ever need to do it.

Although I don't generally advocate making things up, there are circumstances where you might find it helpful to say something like, "My [husband, boyfriend...] is coming just now. He's a [cop, big guy...] and he'll beat you up when he catches you, so you better get out of here fast." Don't hesitate to get creative, but be calm, matter-of-fact and unemotional. This isn't the time to play the drama queen. If you aren't sure how well the guy understands English, speak slowly and use simple words. Come up with a good line and practice it in advance so if you have occasion to use it, you can sound like you really mean it. Smiling confidently will make it more believable and effective.

In a dense crowd, holding your bag in front of you and sticking your elbows out a bit will somewhat reduce the risk of being groped.

## CROWDSOURCING ASSISTANCE

There are many crowded situations in India, many of which you may not be able to avoid. However, try to stay away from demonstrations, protests, political rallies and other big crowds where there are mostly men. Holi is a particularly rowdy festival, so don't go out alone then.

If you attend a major religious festival where the crowds are dense, get up and out of the action to a place where you can observe from a safe distance. Look around for a vantage point such as a balcony, a rooftop, or a stairway where there are other women or girls. Don't be shy about asking the locals if you can join them there. Usually, they will be delighted if you do. Not only is it safer, but you can see better than from the midst of the crowd. Big crowds always seem to attract a few men who view them as an opportunity to get in a little groping. They think there's little risk, as they can just fade into the crowd.

Predators like to use crowds as a shield for groping because they think they can get away easily. In a crowd, the best thing is to call him out, if you know who the culprit is.

Keep your voice as strong, commanding and unemotional as possible. Try not to let your anger show. Don't swear or call him names. And don't let him into your personal space by responding to personal comments or throwing any back at him. Instead, call him out loudly in a way that identifies him and what he has done. You might say something like, "You in the black jacket, keep your hands off me!" or "You with the red shirt, please don't insult me like that!" Being the focus of many censorious eyes should make the coward slink off as quickly as possible. Crowdsourcing your defense in this way—even if no one actually does or says anything to help—will almost always put a stop to the harassment.

Even though many people will applaud a woman for taking extreme measures against eve-teasers, remaining calm and civil may gain you more respect from those around you, and thus make them more inclined to help than to merely stand by and enjoy the entertainment. Watching a foreign girl go wild on some guy would undoubtedly be considered highly entertaining by many people.

Don't be shy about asking for help if the situation is more serious. In case help is not immediately forthcoming, call out to someone who looks reasonably intelligent and responsible, e.g. "You in the striped shirt, please call the police!" A specific call to action to an individual will have others looking to that person to do something and it may inspire him or her to act. You can also say, "I am a guest in your country. Please help me." Positioning yourself as a guest is always a good move in India, as guests are traditionally honored and this is an obligation that most people take seriously.

## SAFE DATING

Be discriminating about where you go for evening entertainment and who you go with. Avoid going alone to nightclubs, bars, etc.

If you drink, keep it moderate. Stay sober and in control. Obviously, getting drunk creates plenty of opportunities for men to take advantage of you—as does getting high on drugs.

Have fun, but don't let your guard down when you are in party mode. Never worry about people feeling uncomfortable because you are being cautious. It's your life and your well-being. If they don't like it, maybe it's time to find new friends who actually care about you.

So-called date rape drugs are almost undetectable, and they leave the victim unconscious and defenseless. Never leave your drink or food unattended and don't accept drinks from strangers. Predators have been known to drug cigarettes, too, so if you smoke, bring your own.

If you suddenly begin to feel strange, sick or drunk after only one or two drinks, tell a trusted friend. Ask them to take you to a safe place away from anyone who might have spiked your drink. If you are alone, phone someone you trust to come and get you. Lock yourself in the bathroom if there is no other safe haven.

Don't leave a bar, club or party with any guy you don't know well and aren't completely sure you can trust. Never let any guy pressure or ridicule you into going with him against your better judgment. If someone invades your personal space, ignores your protests, or tries to make you feel bad for resisting his advances, it's time to leave. Be really clear about communicating where your sexual boundaries lie. Be assertive and don't allow yourself to be pushed beyond what is acceptable.

If you meet someone you'd like to know better, arrange to meet him in a safe public place, give him your email, but don't give him your address or phone number. If he turns out to be a complete jerk, you can easily block his emails.

Whenever you go out with someone you don't know well, take a photo of him and send it to a friend. Tell him you want to remember this date and act like it's what you do all the time.

Never let a date put you down or otherwise treat you badly. If he does, just leave. Lack of respect—talking dirty when you aren't inviting it, making hurtful comments, inflicting mental or emotional abuse, or any rough treatment—can easily escalate to something much worse.

In the process of getting to know someone, be alert to these behaviors, which are often indicators of bad intentions: if the guy is controlling or possessive in any way; if he tries to make you feel obligated to him; if he gets angry easily; if he goes much too far out of his way to be nice to you; if he is disparaging or over-critical; if he accuses you of 'teasing' him sexually; if he urges you to get drunk or stoned; or if he tries to isolate you from others. If he does any of these things, it's time to go. If you need to call for help, do it where he can't hear you.

Dating in India is quite a different matter than in the West. For the most part, Indians don't date, or if they do, it's almost always with the intent of marriage. When Indian men date non-Indians, especially white girls, they are often just looking for sex, money and fun—and a certain status it will give them.

If you happen to have a relaxed view of sex and are up for a nice discreet little fling, don't count on the discreet part. Expect him to brag about scoring with a foreign woman, regardless of his promises. If he's not close to home, all the details are likely to be known by everyone in the vicinity within hours, as a result of which there may be a significant increase in harassment, since everyone will assume you are readily available. Incidentally, you should be aware that AIDS/HIV is not uncommon, so appropriate precautions should be taken.

But if you have fallen in love with an Indian man and are serious about him, there are some things you really must consider.

If he really loves you, he will almost certainly want to marry you. For Indians, it's all about marriage. You can feel confident that he is serious if he introduces you to his family. While he might hesitate to introduce you to his family right away, if he keeps making excuses, he probably never will. If he hides you from his family and friends, he is only using you. And once he has had his fun with you, most likely he will marry an Indian girl as per his family's wishes.

A request for money is a clear sign that he's not in love with you. Don't give him money for any reason. If he asks for money or keeps dropping hints, it's time to dump him, no matter what 'need' he cites. Most likely, it's a lie anyway. Give him money once and he won't stop asking for more, just like any beggar on the street. He'll keep using you and exploiting you.

Using you is a kind of abuse, as is treating you disrespectfully. Even such non-violent abuse can put you at risk in more ways than one.

## FIGHTING BACK

Predators like to target women who seem helpless and unaware of what's going on around them, so do your best to always be aware of your surroundings and to cultivate the appearance of being strong and confident.

Using physical means to defend yourself should absolutely be the last resort, but if you get into a situation where you have to defend yourself physically, do it fast, forcefully and decisively. Don't hesitate. Put up a huge struggle and make as much noise as you can. Deploy the pepper spray, jab him in the eye, knee him hard in the groin, stomp on his instep, or whatever you can do to escape.

Some women hesitate to resist because they are afraid of getting hurt, but statistics show that fighting back increases the odds of a positive outcome by around 70%.

Be careful where you take refuge following an incident, especially a serious one. Try not to end up alone with men who might be inspired to take advantage of the situation. Remember that many men have the mindset that if you were assaulted, you must have done something to invite it—and some might be inclined to think that the invitation has just been extended to them.

## IF YOU HAVE TO GO TO THE POLICE

In the unlikely event that you have to report a crime, notify your embassy right away, even before you call the police, if possible.

To report a crime, you have to file an FIR (First Information Report) at the nearest police station, but avoid going there alone. Sometimes the police are reluctant to register an FIR for one reason or another and you may need to be persistent. Note that merely recording the details in a journal is not the same as filing an FIR. When an FIR is filed, the police must start an investigation. Unfortunately, Indian policemen can often be reluctant to file an FIR for rape.

Avoid being alone with policemen. Insist on dealing with a policewoman, or at least having a woman present while you are making your report.

Any time you have to deal with the police, try to remain calm and keep your voice soft. Getting angry or hysterical will invariably make matters worse. Police in India are quite touchy about behavior they consider disrespectful.

# CONCLUSION

Staying safe in India is really not so hard. Most Indian men are not perverts or predators or interested in harassing you in any way. You don't need to be fearful. Be aware of your surroundings. Be sensible and careful, but don't worry.

There is, of course, no absolute truth when it comes to female safety in India. Some places are safer and more welcoming than others. A little advance research can tell you which places to avoid due to high crime rates and drug abuse or bad attitudes towards women.

Respect is essential, but respecting the culture is about much more than just safety. Many doors will open to you that might otherwise remain firmly closed and hidden. And you will find people much more friendly, open and ready to help you. It's one of the keys to experiencing the best of India.

May your time in India be safe and happy!

## ABOUT THE AUTHOR

I am an American woman who has made India my home. JD Viharini is not the name on my passport, but since I like to remain anonymous, I chose a new name. JD Viharini comes from an epithet of Ganga, *Jambu-dvipa-viharini,* which means 'one who wanders around enjoying India'. That's me, for sure! I love India.

Inspired in my twenties by the Vedic literature and traditions of India (Veda means 'Knowledge of Life,' and the Vedas are the basis of Indian religion and culture), I eventually received a Masters degree in Vedic Studies. With this understanding of the roots of the Indian way of life, I began traveling to India more than three decades ago.

After maybe 15 trips to India, in 2003 I decided that India should be my home. During all this time I've traveled extensively throughout the country—mostly solo—by first class, sardine class, and everything in between. I've been sick and learned how to stay well; resided in opulent hotels and lived in poor villages; stayed with traditional families and studied at ashrams. I have learned how to travel and live, happily and comfortably, in this most magnificent of countries, which I now consider home. Now I wish to share what I've learned in order to help others enjoy India to the fullest.